S N A P S H O T S   I N   H I S T O R Y

HIROSHIMA AND NAGASAKI

Fire from the Sky

by Andrew Langley

HIROSHIMA AND NAGASAKI

Fire from the Sky

by Andrew Langley

Content Adviser: Derek Shouba, Adjunct History Professor
and Assistant Provost, Roosevelt University

Reading Adviser: Susan Kesselring, M.A., Literacy Educator,
Rosemount–Apple Valley–Eagan (Minnesota) School District

COMPASS POINT BOOKS
MINNEAPOLIS, MINNESOTA

HIROSHIMA AND NAGASAKI

✦ COMPASS POINT BOOKS

3109 West 50th Street, #115
Minneapolis, MN 55410

Visit Compass Point Books on the Internet at
www.compasspointbooks.com
or e-mail your request to
custserv@compasspointbooks.com

For Compass Point Books
Jennifer VanVoorst, Jaime Martens, XNR Productions, Inc.,
Catherine Neitge, Keith Griffin, and Carol Jones

Produced by White-Thomson Publishing Ltd.
Tel.: 0044 (0)1273 403990
210 High Street, Lewes BN7 2NH

For White-Thomson Publishing
Stephen White-Thomson, Brian Krumm, Amy Sparks, Tinstar Design
Ltd. *www.tinstar.co.uk*, Derek Shouba, Joselito F. Seldera, Bill Hurd,
and Timothy Griffin

Library of Congress Cataloging-in-Publication Data
Langley, Andrew.
   Hiroshima and Nagasaki : fire from the sky / by Andrew Langley.
      p. cm. — (Snapshots in history)
   Includes bibliographical references and index.
   ISBN 0-7565-1621-8
   1. Hiroshima-shi (Japan)—History—Bombardment, 1945—Juvenile
literature. 2. Nagasaki-shi (Japan)—History—Bombardment, 1945—
Juvenile literature. 3. Atomic bomb—History—Juvenile literature. I.
Title. II. Series.
   D767.25.H6L33 2005
   940.54'2521954—dc22   2005027146

Copyright © 2006 by Compass Point Books
All rights reserved. No part of this book may be reproduced without
written permission from the publisher. The publisher takes no
responsibility for the use of any of the materials or methods described
in this book, nor for the products thereof.
Printed in the United States of America.

HIROSHIMA AND NAGASAKI

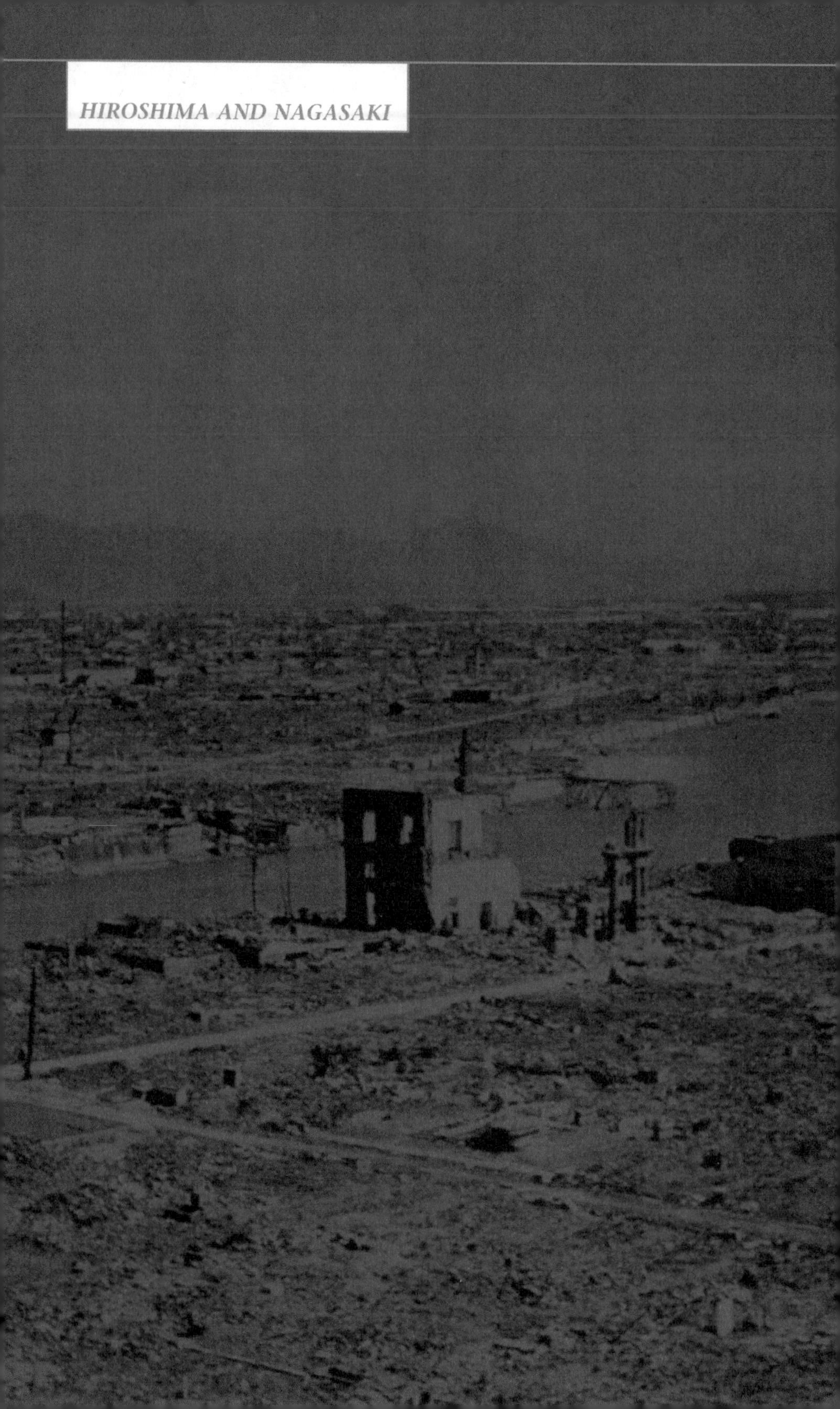

CONTENTS

Fire from the Sky

Chapter

1

The morning of August 6, 1945, was still and cloudless. By 7 A.M., the Japanese port of Hiroshima was bustling with the normal sights and sounds of a new day. People dressed, ate breakfast, and made their way to work—on foot or by bicycle, bus, or streetcar. Massed ranks of soldiers sweated through their exercise routines on the parade grounds of Hiroshima Castle. In the docks, cargo ships were being unloaded.

But life was far from normal. This was wartime, and the city had already been attacked by American bomber aircraft. About 8,000 schoolchildren were helping to tear down houses damaged by the raids. At 7:09 A.M., the wail of a siren warned that an enemy plane was in the area, and people ran for the safety of bomb shelters. But the bomber soon disappeared.

Before its destruction on August 6, 1945, Hiroshima, Japan, was a bustling city.

At 7:31 A.M., the siren sounded the all-clear signal to indicate that there was no longer any danger. Everyone emerged and continued their jobs.

However, 6 miles (10 kilometers) overhead another U.S. Air Force B-29 bomber was also headed for Hiroshima. This one had orders to attack the city.

The pilot, Colonel Paul Tibbets, had called the aircraft *Enola Gay,* and the name was painted in large letters near the cockpit. Suddenly Tom Ferebee, the bombardier of the *Enola Gay,* shouted: "I see it!"

Far below the plane was the city of Hiroshima. Ferebee could see the river that was crossed by a T-shaped bridge at the center of the city. That was the target.

The aircraft thundered on, and at 8:15 A.M., a huge object weighing 9,000 pounds (4,050 kilograms) fell from the bomb bay underneath the plane. It was nicknamed Little Boy, and it was set to explode in 43 seconds.

On the ground in Hiroshima, several people saw the *Enola Gay.* A teacher noticed the airplane, and her students looked up at the sky, too. One student remembered:

> *At that moment, we felt a tremendous flash of lightning. In an instant we were blinded.*

10

A dockyard worker saw: "a flame that was even brighter than the sun."

Colonel Paul Tibbets named his B-29 bomber the Enola Gay, *after his mother.*

An office worker saw:

> *a golden lightning flash which had blown up out of the earth.*

Little Boy exploded about 2,000 feet (610 meters) above the city. Within a split second, it produced a gigantic fireball so hot that the temperature directly underneath it reached 5,400 °F (2,982 °C). The flash of heat brought instant death to almost everyone within half a mile. Their skin was scorched to carbon and their internal organs boiled away. Birds turned to ash in midair. Even people 2 miles (3 km) from the center of the blast suffered severe burns on exposed flesh.

In that same second, the blinding brightness of the light acted like a giant camera. Three thousand times more powerful than sunlight, it bleached the surfaces of the city. The shadows of people, carts, ladders, telegraph poles, and leaves created dark patches that stood out against the whitened materials beneath them. Black parts of clothing burned more

EYEWITNESS IN THE SKY

Sergeant Bob Caron, tail gunner of the *Enola Gay*, made a voice recording as he witnessed the explosion after the bomb was dropped on Hiroshima:

A column of smoke is rising fast. It has a fiery red core ... here it comes, the mushroom shape ... It's like a mass of bubbling molasses. The mushroom is spreading out. It's maybe a mile or two wide and half a mile high. It's growing up and up and up. It's nearly level with us and climbing. The base of the mushroom looks like a heavy undercast that is shot through with flames. The city must be below that.

easily than light ones, leaving grotesque patterns on the wearer's skin. Anyone who looked directly at the flash suffered permanent damage to his or her eyes.

A few moments after the light and heat came the shockwaves caused by the explosion. From the center of the blast, the waves shot outward at 2 miles (3 km) per second like an unbelievably powerful wind.

One schoolgirl later said:

I felt as though I had been struck on the back with something like a big hammer, and thrown into boiling oil.

A mushroom cloud soared above Hiroshima, just minutes after the atomic bomb exploded.

13

A boy was blown out of his house and across the street, passing through two windows on the way. His body was filled with glass fragments.

High above, the *Enola Gay* circled over the city, as the crew watched the horror unfolding. They saw an enormous fireball and felt the shockwaves, which made the aircraft bounce in midair. Then out of the blast a mushroom cloud boiled up into the sky above Hiroshima. Captain Robert Lewis, the co-pilot, said that he could somehow feel the atomic explosion in his mouth. It tasted like lead.

Hiroshima was not the only city that experienced the horror of the fire from the sky. Nagasaki, a Japanese port town would soon feel the devastating effects of the atomic bomb.

The bomb dropped on Hiroshima flattened nearly every building in the city.

Splitting the Atom

Chapter

2

The bombs that fell on Japan in 1945 hurled the world into a new age of warfare. The atomic bomb was the most terrible and murderous weapon ever used in human history, before or since. With the strength of about 20,000 tons (18,100 metric tons) of ordinary high explosives, it produced a blast equal to more than 200 of the biggest bombs used in World War II detonating all at once. The aftereffects were even more devastating.

Little Boy was the first atomic bomb. Its power came from atoms—the tiny particles that make up everything in the universe. An atom is a million times smaller than the width of a human hair, yet it can contain an enormous amount of energy. This energy was harnessed by the makers of the bomb, with the result that a

Leading U.S. scientist Commander Francis Birch made final adjustments to Little Boy, the bomb that was dropped on Hiroshima.

17

big city and most of its people could be wiped out within a few seconds.

It had taken a very long time for scientists to understand the astonishing truth about atomic power. More than 2,400 years ago, a Greek writer named Democritus developed and put forward the idea that all matter was made up of countless particles. He called these particles *atoms,* which meant "things which cannot be split." His theory seemed to be correct, but nobody could prove it.

Many centuries later, scientists added to the theory. In the 1750s, the Croatian Rudjer Boscovich suggested that atoms were not really the smallest units in the universe, but that they contained even tinier particles. In 1897 the British physicist Joseph John Thomson discovered one of these particles, which he called the electron. In 1911 Ernest Rutherford, who was born in New Zealand, found another. This was the nucleus—a particle at the center of the atom.

To understand atoms, the next scientific step was to break one up. But what kind of tool could do this? Amazingly, the answer was other atoms.

THE END OF THE WORLD?

Yoko Ata was a Japanese writer who survived the bombing of Hiroshima. Thinking back about the day Little Boy was dropped, he said:

There was a fearful silence which made one feel that all trees and vegetation were dead ... I thought it might have been something which had nothing to do with the war, the collapse of the earth which it was said would take place at the end of the world.

Some substances are made up of atoms that are naturally unstable. This means that they are always changing and shooting out a stream of particles, including electrons and parts of the nucleus.

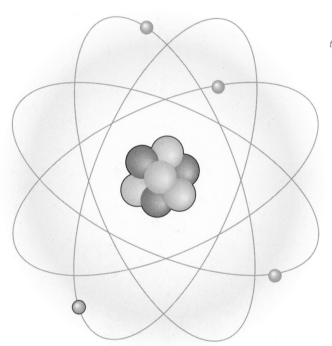

The atom was originally thought to be the smallest unit of matter.

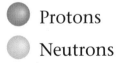 Protons

Neutrons

This process is called radioactivity. Scientists discovered that they could use these flying particles as miniature bullets, firing them at the atoms they wanted to split.

19

Scientist Otto Hahn
was responsible for
groundbreaking work
in atomic physics.

Step by step, they developed ways of
bombarding atoms with radioactive particles.
These pioneers of atomic physics did not imagine

that their discoveries would have any practical use. They were simply trying to understand how the building blocks of matter were put together. But their work was about to change the world forever.

In 1938, the German scientist Otto Hahn and his colleagues announced the result of a series of experiments. They had bombarded uranium (a very radioactive element) with particles called neutrons. This had caused some surprising changes to the uranium and produced barium, an entirely different element.

PARTS OF THE ATOM

Scientists now know that an atom is made up of three kinds of tiny particles. Two of these—the protons and the neutrons—are bunched together tightly in the center. These form the nucleus of the atom. The third kind of particle is the electron. Electrons whiz around the empty space outside the nucleus. An atom of hydrogen contains one proton and one electron, but no neutrons. An atom of uranium contains 92 protons, 146 neutrons, and 92 electrons.

A year later, Austrian physicists Lise Meitner and Otto Frisch studied Hahn's results. They showed that the atoms in the uranium had actually been split.

That was not all. The process of fission, or splitting, had given out more energy than it had used. The incredible power inside the atom had been unlocked.

This was sensational news. Scientists realized that they had discovered a source of power that could be far greater than anything ever invented before. When the neutrons split one atom, it released energy plus more neutrons. These neutrons shot off to split neighboring atoms, which themselves gave off more neutrons.

The fission and the release of energy would go on increasing as long as there were atoms to split. The result of such a chain reaction must be a gigantic explosion.

At this time, nobody knew exactly how big the explosion might be, or how it might be started or controlled. One thing was certain, however: Somebody was going to find out very soon. Whomever built the first atomic bomb would possess the most terrifying of all weapons. ◣

In 1955, physicist Lise Meitner was awarded the first-ever Otto Hahn Prize, for Chemistry and Physics. The award was named after the Nobel Prize-winning physicist whose work laid the foundation for her own remarkable discoveries.

The World at War

3

In 1939, the world was on the brink of a new global war. World War I (1914–1918) had been responsible for the deaths of about 10 million soldiers, and probably just as many people who were not fighting. Many of these people were killed by new weapons of mass destruction—machine guns, highly explosive shells, poison gas, and bombing from the air. Europe had never recovered from the war, and now a second world war was about to begin.

Germany, shamed and ruined by the country's defeat in World War I, had suffered very badly. But in 1933, the Germans elected a new government led by Adolf Hitler and his Nazi Party. Backed by a brutal army and secret police force, Hitler soon became the country's dictator. He imprisoned his enemies, crushed his

Adolf Hitler saluted in triumph to the crowds as he arrived in Saarbrucken, on the German border with France, in October 1938.

opponents, and promised to make Germany feared once again, extending its borders and creating a mighty new armed force.

Another nation had also begun building a new empire. The Japanese had invaded the northern part of China in 1931. Six years later, Japanese

At the beginning of the 1930s, Japan was a country in conflict. In 1936, there was a revolt, and three important members of the civilian government were killed. Military leaders began to expand Japan's army, navy, and air force very rapidly. Rival politicians were bullied into silence or killed. In 1940, Japan joined the fascist states of Germany and Italy in a three-way pact.

leaders began further conquests, seizing the Chinese cities of Peking (now Beijing) and Shanghai. Their aim was to make Japan the most powerful country in Asia—and then in the entire Pacific Ocean region.

By 1939, the rush toward a worldwide conflict seemed unstoppable. Hitler had already started to expand his empire by occupying Austria and then seizing most of the neighboring territory of Czechoslovakia. Now he was threatening to invade Poland, a move that would force Great Britain and France to declare war on Germany.

Against this background, the discovery of the staggering power of nuclear fission became even more important. The race was on to build an atomic bomb and gain an unbeatable advantage in the coming world war.

At this stage, Germany seemed to be well ahead in the race. It had a major supply of uranium, the raw material for a chain reaction. Furthermore, many of the world's greatest physicists were German or Austrian, and much of the pioneering work on splitting the atom had been done by those physicists.

But Hitler had already made a huge mistake. He hated Jewish people and passed a series of new laws that robbed the Jews of their legal rights. By 1939, as the persecution grew more savage, more than 60 percent of all Jews living in Germany had fled to other countries such as England, France, and the United States.

Among them were some of the giants of European science. These included Hans Bethe, Lise Meitner, Leo Szilard, and Edward Teller, who had all done vital work in uncovering the secrets of atomic physics.

In the late 1930s, thousands of Jewish people fled Germany to nearby countries.

The scientist Albert Einstein's theories inspired the development of nuclear physics.

The most famous Jewish scientist was Albert Einstein, whose theory of relativity had made it possible to figure out how much energy might be released in a chain reaction. Fired from his position

at a German university because he was Jewish, he moved to the United States to continue his work at the Institute for Advanced Study in Princeton, New Jersey. On the brink of World War II in August 1939, Einstein was spending the summer on Long Island, New York.

One day Einstein was visited by scientists Leo Szilard and Edward Teller. Szilard already had a horrifying vision of what nuclear fission could cause. He wrote:

> *There was very little doubt in my mind that the world was headed for grief.*

The pair urged Einstein to send a letter to Franklin D. Roosevelt, the president of the United States, warning him of the enormous dangers that would be posed by the development of the atomic bomb by an enemy of the United States. Einstein wrote the letter and suggested that Roosevelt should provide funds to speed up U.S. research work.

But the Germans were also pushing ahead with their work on nuclear weapons. Scientists in Berlin planned to set up a chain reaction using uranium and were certain that the splitting of the atom could be used to destroy entire cities. British spies in Europe sent back alarming news of German progress. The program, however, was doomed to fail. Hitler simply could not see how important it was, and he did not support his researchers.

29

Albert Einstein encouraged the United States to speed up atomic research.

Hitler also thought that other weapons programs would produce better weapons that his soldiers could use sooner in the war. The Nazis would never

The United States has only very poor ores of uranium in moderate quantities. There is some good ore in Canada and the former Czechoslovakia, while the most important source of uranium is Belgian Congo.

In view of this situation you may think it desirable to have some permanent contact maintained between the Administration and the group of physicists working on chain reactions in America. One possible way of achieving this might be for you to entrust with this task a person who has your confidence and who could perhaps serve in an inofficial capacity. His task might comprise the following:

a) to approach Government Departments, keep them informed of the further development, and put forward recommendations for Government action, giving particular attention to the problem of securing a supply of uranium ore for the United States;

b) to speed up the experimental work,which is at present being carried on within the limits of the budgets of University laboratories, by providing funds, if such funds be required, through his contacts with private persons who are willing to make contributions for this cause, and perhaps also by obtaining the co-operation of industrial laboratories which have the necessary equipment.

I understand that Germany has actually stopped the sale of uranium from the Czechoslovakian mines which she has taken over. That she should have taken such early action might perhaps be understood on the ground that the son of the German Under-Secretary of State, von Weizsäcker, is attached to the Kaiser-Wilhelm-Institut in Berlin where some of the American work on uranium is now being repeated.

Yours very truly,

A. Einstein

(Albert Einstein)

develop an atomic bomb, though the British and the Americans did not know this in the early days of World War II.

The government and most people in the United States had been determined to stay out of the war. Most people in the United States thought that the war was only a concern for Europe and North Africa.

However on the morning of December 7, 1941, two great waves of Japanese aircraft swooped down on the Pacific fleet of the United States at Pearl Harbor in Hawaii. The raids killed 2,403 Americans and damaged or destroyed 21 ships and about 347 aircraft.

LETTER TO THE PRESIDENT

Albert Einstein wrote a letter to President Roosevelt on August 2, 1939. Part of the letter reads:

In the course of the last four months it has been made probable ... that it may become possible to set up a nuclear chain reaction in a large mass of uranium, by which vast amounts of power would be generated. Now it appears almost certain that this could be achieved in the immediate future. This new phenomenon would also lead to the construction of bombs. A single bomb of this type, carried by a boat and exploded in a port, might very well destroy the whole port together with some of the surrounding territory.

On the evening of December 7, 1941, Japan formally declared war on Great Britain and the United States. On December 8, President Roosevelt spoke of the Pearl Harbor attack to the U.S. Congress. Later that day, the United States declared war on Japan. The United States was now part of the massive conflict, which had split the world in two. Most nations supported either the Allies (which included Great Britain, the Soviet Union, Australia, and the United States) or the Axis powers (which included Germany, Japan, and Italy).

Japanese forces made lightning progress. They advanced into Southeast Asia and the Western Pacific. Within four months, they had conquered Indonesia, Malaya, and most of Burma, and

Clouds of smoke billowed from U.S. battleships hit during the Japanese attack on Pearl Harbor on December 7, 1941.

invaded the Philippines, the Solomon Islands, and New Guinea. Their aircraft dropped bombs on northern Australia, while Japanese midget submarines attacked ships inside Sydney Harbor.

Some of the Japanese attack expeditions began in the port city of Hiroshima. It was one of the most important cities in the southwest region of Japan. Hiroshima had once been the country's

President Roosevelt signed the declaration of war against Japan on December 8, 1941.

capital, and by the outbreak of the war, it was a vital center for industry and the armed forces. It was the headquarters of a division of Japan's army, a major storage depot, and the city where soldiers assembled before being shipped out to Asia and the Pacific. A Japanese reporter wrote:

> *More than a thousand times did the Hiroshima citizens see off with cries of "Banzai" the troops leaving from the harbor.*

Another important military center was the Japanese port city of Nagasaki, on the southernmost island of Kyushu. It boasted several factories making much-needed weapons for Japan's armed forces. The importance of Hiroshima and Nagasaki to Japan's military capabilities was something U.S. officials would consider later in the war. ◣

The Race for the Bomb

Chapter

4

T he explosion of Japanese power into the war posed a terrifying threat for the Allies. But by the spring of 1942, the Americans were retaliating. In April, U.S. bombers made their first raid on Tokyo. The raid did little damage, but showed the Japanese leaders that their homeland was not safe from attack. Then the U.S. Navy stopped the Japanese advance with two vital victories in the Pacific area, at the battles of the Coral Sea and Midway.

Meanwhile, in Washington, D.C., President Roosevelt had given the go-ahead for a large-scale official program of research into uranium-based weapons in late 1941. Politicians now recognized that winning the race to build an atomic bomb might also mean winning the war. The Allies were driven by a dreadful fear that their enemies might get there before them.

Repeated American bombing raids crippled most Japanese cities. Japanese soldiers retaliated by firing on American planes from rooftops.

In May 1942, an American official, James B. Conant, gave an alarming report on German progress, using the evidence sent to him by secret agents:

> *If they are hard at work, they cannot be far behind us. There are still plenty of competent scientists left in Germany. They may be ahead of us by as much as a year.*

Were the Japanese also close to building a bomb? They had started a study in 1941 but had not made much progress because there was little government support. The Japanese navy thought that nuclear energy could only practically be used to power its ships. However, a physicist named Tokutaro Hagiwara believed that a nuclear chain reaction might set off a giant explosion, and he was working hard on more research at the University of Kyoto. The Allies could not afford to waste any time in making their own weapon.

In September 1942, Colonel Leslie R. Groves was appointed to lead the American atomic project. At first, he was angry to be stuck in home territory. He knew nothing about the bomb program, which was still top secret. Most of the research was being done at Columbia University in New York, and the organization was being run from an office in Manhattan (which is why it soon became known as the "Manhattan Project"). Groves had been looking forward to a posting overseas where the action was. "I don't want to stay in Washington," he told his senior officer.

The general's reply gave him no choice:

> *If you do the job right, it will win the war.*

Groves was stunned. He quickly got over his disappointment and showed he had a ruthless kind of energy that got things done. Knowing little about physics, he insisted that a scientist should direct the project. He chose Robert Oppenheimer, whom he described as "a real genius." His next job was to find a big enough supply of uranium for the scientists to work on. A large supply of the material was discovered in a warehouse on Staten Island, New York.

Born in the United States and educated at Harvard University, Robert Oppenheimer was one of the first scientists to research black holes in space.

39

Groves immediately sent someone to buy the uranium and move it to Chicago where Nobel-Prize-winning physicist Enrico Fermi would perform an experiment with it.

Chicago was the scene for the next great moment in the history of the atomic bomb. In November 1942, Fermi began to build the world's first nuclear reactor in a little-used squash court at the University of Chicago. This would prove once and for all that a chain reaction could produce enough energy for a vast explosion. Just as important, the experiment would show that the chain reaction could be controlled.

To construct the nuclear reactor, workers stacked graphite blocks in the shape of a circular pile. The blocks had small spheres of radioactive uranium in them. The graphite slowed down the radioactivity of the uranium. Even so, as the pile grew higher, the energy caused by the escaping radioactive particles grew greater. The scientists pushed special "control rods" into the pile to stop the radioactivity altogether.

On December 2, 1942, the stack was 57 layers high. The team began to pull out the control rods one by one. Slowly, the pile came to life as the neutrons became active. Machines recorded each escaping neutron, clicking every time one was counted. The clicks came faster until they merged into a single roar of noise. Fermi raised his hand and said:

The pile has gone critical.

This meant that the experiment was a success. Fermi had created a self-sustaining atomic chain reaction. He also proved that humans could control and use atomic power.

A model was made of the pile Enrico Fermi constructed in a squash court at the University of Chicago in 1942.

It was a moment for huge celebration: The theory of nuclear fission was correct after all. The scientists had not been certain the theory was valid until now. Some of the team, however, were not thrilled. The idea of a giant weapon of mass terror, capable of killing thousands of people, had just become a reality. To a man like Leo Szilard, this was not something to celebrate:

> *I shook hands with Fermi, and I said that I thought this day would go down as a black day in the history of mankind.*

It was clear to Groves and Oppenheimer that something as secret and as dangerous as an atomic bomb could not be built in a big city such as Chicago. They decided to move the Manhattan Project to a new site, far away in the deserts of New Mexico. A laboratory was built at Los Alamos, near Santa Fe. By the summer of 1943, a whole new community had sprung up in this remote area.

Here, Oppenheimer assembled his team, which included some of the most brilliant chemists, physicists, and engineers in the world. Oppenheimer called it:

> *the greatest collection of eggheads ever.*

During 1943 and 1944, they worked on the complicated task of designing and manufacturing the bomb.

42

Meanwhile, World War II was turning in favor of the Allies. Allied troops landed in Italy in 1943 and

in France in 1944 and they steadily drove the
Nazi forces back toward their homeland. Hitler
ordered his soldiers to fight to the death, but
thousands of them surrendered every day.

*The town of Los
Alamos, New
Mexico, grew up
around the
Manhattan
Project lab.*

43

American soldiers flew flags of victory after they captured the city of Nuremberg, Germany, in May 1945.

By April 1945, the German capital of Berlin had been surrounded, and victory was in sight. The final German surrender came on May 7. The war in Europe was over.

THE RACE FOR THE BOMB

In the Pacific, however, progress was much slower. American and Australian forces had driven the Japanese from the jungles of New Guinea and the Solomon Islands and then from the islands of the central Pacific.

These battles were long and bitter, for the Japanese usually refused to surrender, even when defeat was certain. In October 1944, the Allies began their attack on the Philippines, a country controlled by the Japanese. During the six-month campaign, about 350,000 Japanese soldiers died, while the Americans lost about 14,000.

KAMIKAZE ATTACKS

As defeat loomed for Japan in late 1944, young pilots were recruited to fly suicide missions. They took off in aircraft packed with explosives and flew them at American ships, airfields, and even massive B-29 bombers. Others jammed themselves into torpedoes, which were fired from submarines and then steered at the target. These were called *kamikaze* attacks, from a Japanese phrase meaning "divine wind." The suicide campaign caused much damage, with one of every 33 missions sinking an American ship.

By early 1945, it was obvious that the Japanese were beaten. The Allies had won back all the territory that the Japanese had invaded, and they had complete control of the air and the sea. American B-29 bombers were destroying Japan's factories and dock areas, while American submarines were sinking ships that brought food and other essential supplies. A massive bombing raid on Tokyo left the capital city blazing, about 100,000 people dead, and another 1 million without homes.

45

Still, the Japanese refused to quit. That summer, some members of Japan's government argued for a complete surrender, but their views were scorned. Most Japanese soldiers and leaders had been taught to believe that surrender would bring unbearable shame on their families and their country. In the past, Japanese warriors had killed themselves with their own swords rather than be captured by an enemy. Now, many were ready to follow them.

WILL THE JAPANESE SURRENDER?

Joseph C. Grew was an American who lived in Japan during the 1930s. He gave this opinion of the Japanese in 1942:

The Japanese will not crack ... even when eventual defeat stares them in the face. They will pull in their belts another notch, reduce their rations from a bowl of rice to a half bowl of rice, and fight to the bitter end. Only by utter physical destruction or utter exhaustion of their men and materials can they be defeated. That is the difference between the Germans and the Japanese.

Allied leaders began to plan for a final invasion of the Japanese mainland that would take place in November 1945. In front of them was a frightening picture. Even when faced with days of bombing and shelling, followed by the landing of a gigantic force of troops, U.S. officials at the time thought the Japanese would most likely fight on to the bitter end. Thousands—maybe millions—of them would die.

It was estimated that about 1 million Allied soldiers would be killed as well. However, historians today still debate using any of these reasons as justification for the bombings.

The Allies would soon have a way of ending the war, without putting a single one of their soldiers into the battlefield. They were about to create the first atomic bomb. The Allies thought that if they threatened to use this terrible weapon against Japan, the Japanese government would be forced to surrender and the war would be over.

The population of Hiroshima was about 255,000 at the time of the bombings. About 240,000 people lived in Nagasaki.

HIROSHIMA AND NAGASAKI

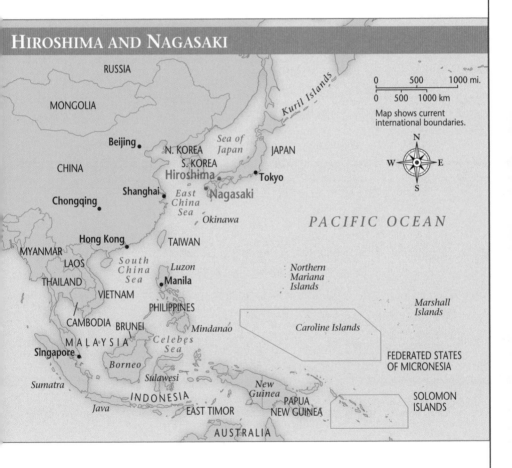

First, the scientists had to prove that the bomb really was as powerful as they thought. By July 1945, members of the Manhattan Project team at Los Alamos were ready to make their final test.

They built a tall steel tower far out in a remote part of the New Mexico desert, and on top of this they slowly assembled the bomb, bit by bit. Then, they were ready to detonate. Some took refuge in nearby bunkers, while others went as far as 20 miles (32 km) away to watch.

Niels Bohr (1885–1962)

Niels Bohr was one of the scientists who worked to construct the world's first nuclear bomb. Born in Denmark, he won the Nobel Prize for Physics in 1922 and was an outstanding pioneer in studying the structure of atoms. He escaped from the Nazis in 1943 and went to the United States, where he joined the project at Los Alamos.

Near dawn on July 16, 1945, the bomb was detonated. The scientists witnessed something no human had ever seen before. Physicist Isidor Rabi wrote:

Suddenly there was an enormous flash of light. It blasted; it pounced, it bored its way right through you. It looked menacing. A new thing had been born.

The fireball reminded Robert Oppenheimer of a line from ancient Hindu scripture:

Now I am become death, the destroyer of worlds.

The test at Los Alamos showed without any doubt that a nuclear explosion caused unbelievable destruction. Most of the steel tower had turned to vapor and had simply disappeared into thin air.

A scientist came to congratulate Leslie Groves. He said: "The war is over."

Groves's reply was chilling: "Yes, after we drop two bombs on Japan."

Leslie Groves (left) and Robert Oppenheimer inspected the remains of the tower that the first atomic bomb had been hung from on July 16, 1945.

At that moment, the leaders of the main Allied nations were arriving for a meeting in Potsdam, Germany. The meeting, known today as the Potsdam Conference, took place from July 17 to August 2, 1945. U.S. President Harry Truman (who had taken over after Franklin D. Roosevelt had died on April 12, 1945) and British Prime Minister Clement Attlee agreed to broadcast a declaration over the radio to Japan. This warned the Japanese government that it must surrender immediately and without any further argument. The broadcast did not mention the atomic bomb but promised "prompt and utter destruction."

Bombing Hiroshima

Japan rejected the terms of the declaration and went on fighting. The Japanese leaders did not know that the parts for the first bombs were already on their way by ship to Tinian, one of the islands in the Marianas Islands near Japan.

Tinian had been recaptured from the Japanese and was now a base for the B-29 bombers of the U.S. Air Force. Among the aircrews stationed there was the one led by Colonel Paul Tibbets, and among the aircraft on the base was the *Enola Gay*.

On July 31, 1945, President Truman ordered the war department in Washington to send a message to the air force commander on Tinian. This gave the final order that the bomb should be dropped.

The message from Truman read:

> *Hiroshima should be given first priority.*

Hiroshima had been on a list of possible targets, but a recent report had shown that it was the only city without an Allied prisoner-of-war camp nearby. No Allies would die in the blast. Hiroshima became the primary U.S. target for the first bombing mission.

President Truman returned from the Potsdam Conference aboard the USS Augusta.

The city of Nagasaki was also considered as a target. Among the factories that produced weapons in Nagasaki was the Mitsubishi factory. This factory had produced the torpedoes used in the devastating attack at Pearl Harbor. The Japanese cities of Kyoto, Yokohama, and Niigata and an arsenal in Kokura were also considered as targets.

Soon the bomb nicknamed "Little Boy" was assembled and ready. On August 3, officers on Tinian called together the crews specially selected for the bombing missions. Until this moment, they had not been told why they were there. Now they found out that they were going to drop the most destructive weapon ever made. It must have seemed to some of them like a strange, frightening dream.

By 8 A.M. on August 6, Colonel Paul Tibbets and his crew of nine men had made their final preparations and pulled on their flak suits, which protected them from flying debris, and dark goggles. They climbed aboard the *Enola Gay* and started down the runway. It was a difficult takeoff, because the B-29 was weighed down with an extra-heavy load—an atomic bomb weighing about 9,000 pounds (4,050 kg) slung in its bomb bay.

With its huge supply of fuel for the long flight, the aircraft weighed more than 65 tons (59 metric tons) in total. The *Enola Gay* was almost at the very end of the runway before it lumbered into the air and set off for Hiroshima.

53

The people of Hiroshima were about to have the most horrifying experience of their lives—one that would end the lives of many of them. The first impact of the lightning flash and the fireball was terrifying enough. Then came the unbelievable force of the shockwaves, crushing buildings and hurling people through the air.

What came next was another form of destruction—fire. The heat flash and the blast started blazes all over the city, which were quickly fanned into a firestorm by the shockwaves and winds that came after them. Many people who survived the first explosion were trapped in shattered houses and burned in the sea of flames. Altogether, about 80,000 of Hiroshima's 255,000 citizens were killed or fatally wounded in the first few seconds after the explosion.

As the *Enola Gay* turned for home after the dropping of the bomb, Captain Robert Lewis was looking down at Hiroshima. He wrote in his flight journal:

My God, what have we done?

A few minutes before the bomb dropped, Hiroshima had been a city of buildings and streets. Now Lewis could barely make out anything except smoke and fire and the enormous mushroom cloud. The explosion flattened everything in its path. More than 62,000 buildings were destroyed, and people were flung about like rags.

The streets of Hiroshima were filled with confusion and horror. People dug their way out of the rubble and tried to find some way to escape. But wherever they went were piles of dead bodies, crowds of victims with scorched skin and clothing, or people writhing in agony. Even in clear areas it was impossible to know where to go because most landmarks had disappeared and the air was thick with dust.

The bomb nicknamed Little Boy exploded over Hiroshima at about 2,000 feet (600 m).

The destruction done to the city of Hiroshima was evident a month after the bombing.

56

In panic, thousands jumped into the rivers that flowed through Hiroshima, seeking some way out from the awful heat. Many of them drowned, and soon the water was choked with corpses, which the current slowly carried away toward the sea. One man even used the bodies as a bridge. He started to crawl across a stream over the corpses on his hands and knees. He was nearly halfway across when a corpse sank beneath him and he had to crawl back to avoid being drowned.

CHILDREN REMEMBER THE BOMBING OF HIROSHIMA

There was a person who had a big splinter of wood stuck in his eye—and he was running around blindly.

a third-grade girl

I was walking among dead people. ... It was like hell.

a 17-year-old girl

No matter where you looked there was nothing but burned people all around.

a first-grade girl

Everybody in the shelter was crying out loud. I don't know how many times I called, begging that they would cut off my burned arms and legs.

a fifth-grade girl

I saw many children ... with dead mothers. ... I just cannot put into words the horror I felt.

a 17-year-old girl

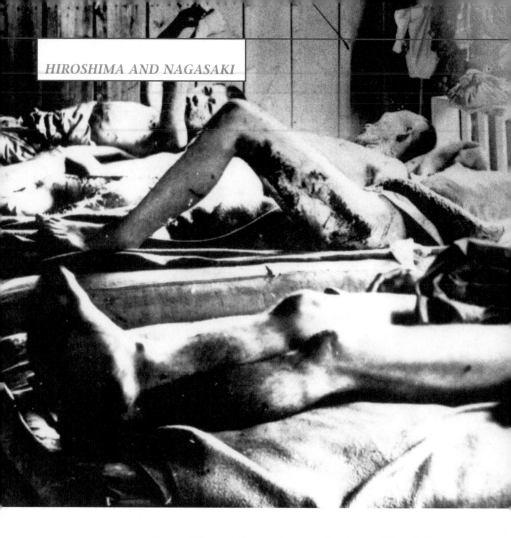

One of the victims who survived was Michihiko Hachiya, a doctor at a Hiroshima hospital. He wrote a diary of what happened on August 6, 1945, and the days that followed.

After the explosion, Hachiya found himself in the ruins of his house, naked and bleeding from several wounds. He staggered into the street, where all around him buildings were swaying and then collapsing. Hachiya wrote:

> *Scorching winds howled around us, whipping dust and ashes into our eyes and up our noses.*

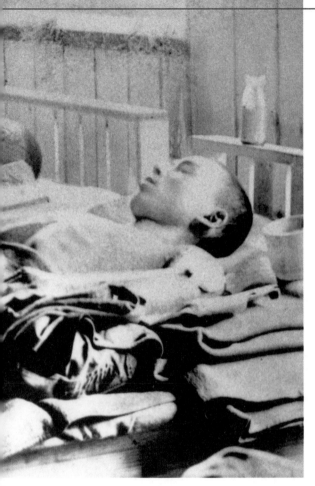

After the bombing, whatever hospital beds and rooms that were not destroyed were overcrowded with sick and wounded people.

Dr. Hachiya headed for his hospital, but he soon fainted. When he woke up, he seemed to be surrounded by walking ghosts. These were people so badly burned that they were holding their arms out to stop the raw flesh from rubbing against their clothes. All were heading for the hospital. But shortly after the doctor reached the hospital, part of it was engulfed in flames. ◣

Death of Two Cities

6

Throughout that day and into the night, the survivors of the Hiroshima bombing struggled to stay alive and bring help to the wounded and dying. Fires still raged, and two-thirds of all of the city's buildings had been destroyed. On top of this, water, electricity, drainage, and other public utilities had been destroyed and could not be used. Most hospitals were damaged, and 90 percent of doctors, nurses, and other medical staff had been killed or badly wounded.

The morning after the bombing, Dr. Hachiya was awakened by fierce sunlight shining through gaping holes where shutters and windows had been blown out. All around him were groaning patients, without food or anyone to attend to them. Outside, things were even more horrific.

The shock and horror of the bomb blast was seen on the faces of survivors of the Hiroshima bombing months after the explosion.

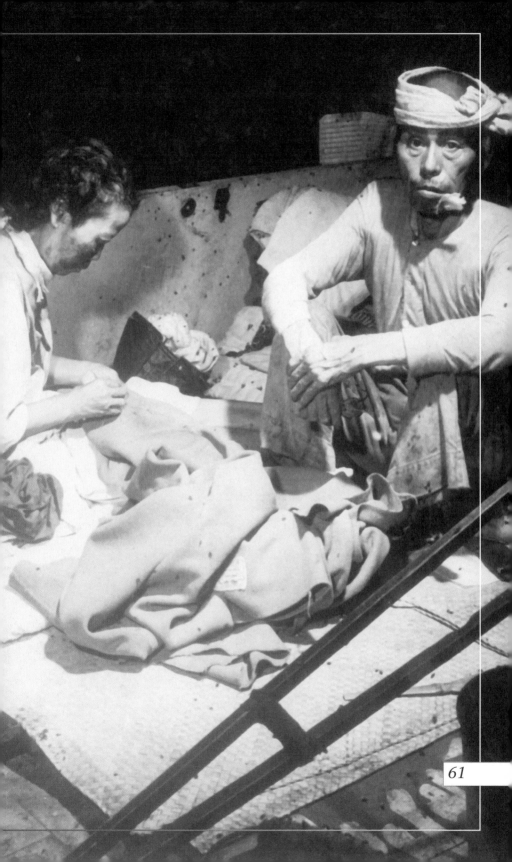

The stench of the dead bodies in Hiroshima was so great that many people wore masks to try to block it.

Visitors told him of long lines of wounded people shuffling through the streets and then dying by the side of the road.

Volunteers began to stack the bodies into big mountains, pour oil on them, and burn them. After a couple of days, however, the task had become impossible. There were too many bodies to be stacked, and the smell of rotting flesh was unbearable. This stench mingled with the smells of fires and dust to produce an odor that reminded Dr. Hachiya of burning sardines.

The great city of Hiroshima had been almost destroyed. This meant that the news of the tragedy did not reach Tokyo, Japan's capital, for many hours. It was not until August 8, 1945, that the Japanese government issued a statement of its disgust. The bombing, it said, would brand the enemy for ages to come as the destroyer of mankind and as public enemy number one of social justice. However, the Japanese leaders could still not agree to surrender.

The Americans tried to spur Japanese leaders to surrender by changing the minds of ordinary Japanese citizens. They dropped leaflets and broadcast messages that said:

> *We are in possession of the most destructive weapon ever designed by man. This is an awful fact for you to ponder. We have just begun to use this weapon against your homeland. If you still have any doubt, ask about what happened to Hiroshima when just one atomic bomb fell on that city. ... We ask that you now petition your Emperor to end the war.*

While the Japanese leaders quarreled about what to do, an operation was already underway to drop a second bomb on Japan. The target chosen was Kokura, a coastal town on the island of Kyushu, southwest of Hiroshima. Kokura was one of Japan's biggest storage areas for weapons and ammunition.

Long before dawn on August 9, three days after the first bombing, another heavily loaded B-29 took off from the U.S. Air Force base on Tinian. The plane was called *Bockscar,* after Frederick Bock, the pilot who usually flew it. On that day, the aircraft was piloted by Major Chuck Sweeney. The bomb's nickname was "Fat Man," because it was much rounder than Little Boy, the bomb that was dropped on Hiroshima. By midmorning, Bockscar was circling high above the north coast of Kyushu.

The weather saved Kokura. The town was covered in low clouds, as well as ground fog and smoke. After circling the town twice, Sweeney decided that he could not see the target area clearly enough and would carry on to the secondary target. His aircraft was low on fuel, and he could not afford to wait. So he turned away and flew southward toward the city of Nagasaki.

With a population of about 240,000, Nagasaki was one of Japan's oldest and biggest ports and home to a large number of Japanese Christians. It was also an important center of shipbuilding and other industries, including a weapons factory. On this fateful morning, the city was also covered in clouds, and Sweeney had to consider giving up the mission altogether and dropping his very expensive cargo into the sea on the way home.

Aircrew studied a map of Nagasaki before setting off to drop the second atomic bomb.

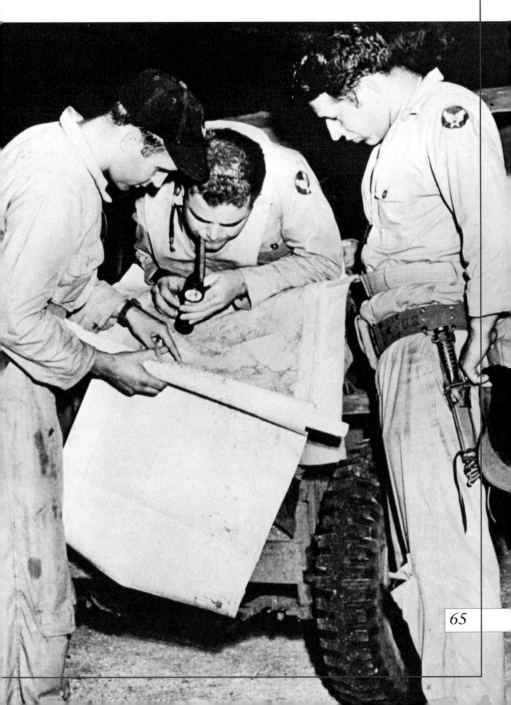

However, the clouds suddenly parted, and at about 11 A.M., Fat Man was dropped from the bomb bay of *Bockscar*. It exploded about 1,650 feet (500 m) above Nagasaki. An American journalist in another aircraft later described the scene in a report:

Fat Man's explosion over Nagasaki created a dense atomic cloud.

> *The giant flash, followed by a bluish green light that filled the sky, and the shockwaves made the bomber tremble from nose to tail.*

Next came a fireball, leaping up with such enormous speed that it reached the height of the B-29 in only 45 seconds. The journalist continued:

> *Awe-struck we watched the pillar of fire shoot upward like a meteor coming from the earth instead of from outer space. It was no longer smoke or dust or even a cloud of fire, it was a living thing.*

Finally, the reporter saw the giant mushroom cloud boiling out of the top of the fireball. Fat Man had detonated with an even greater force than had Little Boy, but it actually caused less damage to the buildings of the city. Hiroshima had been a very flat site, so the blast had traveled straight outward from the center.

However, Nagasaki had many steep hills around it, which absorbed some of the shock and stopped the blast from traveling so far. Even so, the blast immediately killed or mortally wounded about 45,000 people.

Amazingly, several survivors from the Hiroshima disaster had recently arrived in Nagasaki. One of them, a ship designer, was trying to convince his boss of the enormous power of the bomb that had been used there. His boss refused to believe that a single weapon could destroy a city and told the designer that the blast had affected his brain. At that moment there was the mighty flash of the second explosion. The man hurled himself under a desk, followed swiftly by his boss.

Only one building remained standing amid the ruins of Nagasaki after the bombing.

The horrors of Hiroshima were repeated in Nagasaki. Only a few hundred people had taken refuge in the underground bomb shelters. Anyone who was within about 1,000 yards (914 m) of the

blast was burned to ash within seconds, while those farther away had their skin scorched, raising huge blisters. Many others were hit by flying rubble or trapped in collapsing houses. Many fires broke out, but there was no firestorm as there had been at Hiroshima.

That evening the Japanese government began yet again to discuss surrendering. Their meeting was held in an underground bunker in Tokyo, because nowhere in Japan was one safe from the threat of nuclear attack. Even now, the military leaders did not want to give in. They would rather die than endure the shame of surrender.

HOW THE BOMBS WORKED

Little Boy and Fat Man were not the same type of atomic bomb, and they worked in different ways. The first bomb contained uranium. It was detonated by firing one piece of uranium into another, which started a chain reaction. The second bomb contained plutonium, which is even more radioactive than uranium. This was surrounded by explosives. When they exploded, they squashed the plutonium from all sides, causing an immediate chain reaction.

On August 9, 1945, Japan's Emperor Hirohito gave a speech to his war council in which he said:

> *I cannot bear to see my innocent people struggle any longer. Ending the war is the only way to restore world peace and to relieve the nation from the terrible distress with which it is burdened.*

The others accepted his advice, and next morning agreed to surrender—with one condition. They refused to allow the Allies to take away any power from the emperor.

U.S. President Truman refused to agree to this condition. The emperor would have to be under the control of the Allied leaders.

At the same time, Truman secretly gave orders to stop the atomic bombing. He said that the thought of wiping out another 100,000 people was too horrible. Even so, B-29s went on bombing Japanese cities with ordinary high-explosive bombs.

Emperor Hirohito retained his people's support, and they cheered when he appeared in public.

Once again, Emperor Hirohito persuaded his ministers to concede. On August 14, 1945, Emperor Hirohito called a meeting of his war council and told them that he wanted Japan to surrender. No one argued with his decision. At midday on August 15, Hirohito made a radio broadcast to his people to announce the surrender. Few of them had ever heard his voice before.

In Hiroshima, Dr. Hachiya and his colleagues gathered around the hospital radio. A doctor near the radio set heard it all. He turned to the others and said:

> *We've lost the war.*

Many refused to believe it. Until that moment they had thought that Japan was actually winning. Hachiya later wrote:

> *The hospital suddenly turned into an uproar, and there was nothing anybody could do.*

Hachiya wrote that people became desperate—they had lost their families, their friends, and their homes, and now they had lost their pride.

Out of the Ruins

Chapter

7

The people who survived the first few days after the bombing of Hiroshima and Nagasaki thought the worst was over. Many began to recover from their wounds. But soon a new and even more sinister horror appeared. This was radiation sickness—the result of the deadly rays that were released by the fission of the uranium and plutonium atoms in the bombs.

At his hospital in Hiroshima, Dr. Hachiya was glad to see that the number of people dying started to drop about one week after the blast. But then he noticed that many of his patients were developing patches of tiny purple spots under the skin. He did not know what caused them. In some, the number of spots began to increase. Their hair fell out and they grew

Emergency relief organizations offered rice balls to survivors of the bombings, many of whom suffered from starvation and radiation sickness.

weaker and thinner every day. Almost everyone suffered from diarrhea or vomiting.

Slowly the death rate at the hospital began to rise again. People who had been near the center of the blast and escaped injury now became ill, and so did many who had been much farther away. Some died within two days, but nearly all of them died within one week. Doctors in Hiroshima and Nagasaki gradually realized that they were seeing a

With their city and possessions reduced to rubble, most survivors had very little to remind them of their former lives.

completely new kind of disease, which at first they called "atomic bomb illness."

The radiation had other horrifying effects. All the pregnant women who were within 3,000 feet (910 m) of the blast lost their babies. Others farther away had babies who died soon after they were born. Many men became sterile and could not father children for several months after the explosion.

RADIATION SICKNESS

The particles and rays that are given off by a nuclear explosion are very high in energy. People who are exposed to them are very likely to develop radiation sickness. The rays cause damage to cells in the body, especially sensitive ones such as the cells that produce bone marrow and other vital parts of the blood. This often causes a drop in the number of white blood cells, and without these the human body cannot fight infections.

For those who survived the blast and the radiation sickness, life was still horrible. Not only their buildings but also their community had been destroyed. Hospitals, schools, police stations, restaurants, shops, theaters, temples, and offices no longer existed. Most private things that comfort people had also disappeared, from pets and toys to personal letters, gardens, and family treasures.

Many people felt completely lost and helpless. One Hiroshima author wrote:

> *We were being killed against our will by something completely unknown to us. It is the misery of being thrown into a world of new terror and fear, a world more unknown than that of people sick with cancer.*

75

Still, life began to return to the flattened streets of Hiroshima and Nagasaki very quickly. Thousands of people had run away to the hills immediately after the bomb had exploded. Now they came back, each looking for the patch of land where their home had once stood. On August 31, 1945, Hiroshima's local newspaper went on sale in the city once again. On September 10, the supply of electricity was repaired in several areas.

Teachers and children returned to class not long after the bombing, with the city of Hiroshima visible through glassless windows.

76

Help from other countries and organizations also began to arrive in the two devastated cities. The Japanese government distributed supplies of free emergency food rations and set up makeshift hospitals. Soldiers were sent from Tokyo to clear the worst of the rubble and dead bodies. Soon after this, 24 new government offices were opened to sell food. The Hiroshima city government announced that it would give free building materials to anyone who asked. A little town of wooden huts took form just outside the center of the city.

In January 1946, a new government department began work in Hiroshima. Its task was to plan the rebuilding of the city in a modern way, with wide straight avenues instead of the old, narrow, winding streets and open parks instead of tiny gardens. But first, the department had to face a big question—should the new city be built somewhere else, away from the scorched and poisoned desert where the old one had stood?

A few weeks later, as spring arrived, something miraculous happened that gave them an answer. Near the Town Hall were two cherry trees. They looked blackened and dead, ready to be cut down for firewood like all the other trees in the city. Then, one morning in April, they began to blossom with the white flowers that the Japanese especially love.

Hundreds of people came to look at this miracle, which showed beyond doubt that new life could spring up again in the ruins of Hiroshima.

Workers dug gardens near new one-story houses in Hiroshima in March 1946.

By the summer of 1946, large parts of the city were alive again. People, desperate for food, dug or plowed any patch of bare earth and planted it with crops. Potatoes, tomatoes, cabbages, and even rice were grown where the town center had once been.

American troops gave out bags of cornmeal to try to feed the people of Hiroshima. But most Japanese people had never seen cornmeal before. Even with U.S. aid, thousands went hungry.

August 6, 1946, was the first anniversary of what the citizens now called the *pikadon*—a Japanese word referring to the "flash-boom" of the atomic bomb's explosion. The people of Hiroshima placed thousands of white lanterns in the Ohta River, which carried them away to the sea. Each lantern was marked with the name of someone who was dead or missing.

In 1947, the second anniversary was observed in a much grander way. It was called the "Festival of

Peace," and lasted for three days. The streets were filled with the noise of singing, dancing, processions, and fireworks. Two Buddhist priests chanted prayers for the victims from a wooden tower that was built for the festival.

Meanwhile, the reconstruction of Hiroshima and Nagasaki was going very slowly, despite the efforts of the city governments. There was simply not enough money to pay for the materials and the people who would do the work. It was not until 1948 that Shinzo Hamai, the mayor of Hiroshima, started a campaign called "Help Hiroshima." Supported by people from all sections of the community, he took his cause to the Japanese parliament in Tokyo, begging them for more money.

Finally, on May 11, 1949, the parliament passed a law declaring that Hiroshima was to be called "The City of Peace." Hiroshima would have a special importance in Japan and be given large sums to help with rebuilding. Not surprisingly, this angered the people of Nagasaki. Why should Hiroshima get special treatment and not them? Another law was quickly passed, giving Nagasaki the title of "City of International Culture" and a smaller grant of money.

Now major work could begin. Armies of workers moved into the centers of both cities, demolishing wooden shacks, clearing away rubble, and digging the foundations for new streets and apartment blocks. One of the first buildings to be completed in Hiroshima was a new baseball stadium.

In October 1949, a new chill fell across Japan. Leaders in the Soviet Union announced that they had built and tested their first atomic bomb. Now the United States and the Soviet Union—the two strongest countries in the world—both had nuclear weapons. Certainly there was a new worldwide struggle going on, this time between the developing communist countries (backed by Russia and China) and the capitalist countries of the West (backed by the United States). This conflict flared up in Korea, just northwest of Japan. Communist troops from North Korea invaded South Korea, a U.S. ally, in a war that would last three years.

Even though the Korean War was a dangerous time for the whole world, it was very good for Hiroshima. The soldiers fighting communists in Korea came from many countries, and all of them belonged to the United Nations (U.N.). Hiroshima was the perfect place for U.N. forces to buy their equipment and supplies. Before World War II, it had been a major center for weapons factories, and the old plants were now rebuilt to meet the new demand for weapons. Over the next three years, Hiroshima quickly grew rich. New houses, office blocks, streets, parks, railways, and other services were completed. At night the city was vibrant with neon advertising, brightly lit bars, and noisy bazaars.

The money was also spent on something even more important. A Garden of Peace was laid out on an island in the Ohta River, linked to the mainland by a Bridge of Peace. At one end of the garden

The rebuilt Nagasaki today looks peaceful and prosperous in its beautiful waterside setting.

stood the Atomic Bomb Dome, the remains of one of the few buildings not destroyed by the blast. At the other end, the Memorial to the Atomic Victims was erected. It was a simple canopy in the style of old Japanese houses, with the simple inscription:

> *Rest in peace. The mistake shall never be made again.*

In Nagasaki, a Peace Park was constructed as a memorial. There, a giant statue stands, with its right hand pointing upward. It is a permanent warning to be on guard against destruction from the sky.

The Shadow of the Bomb

Chapter

8

The war in Korea clearly showed how the world had divided into two new camps after World War II. The communist Soviet Union and the capitalist United States headed the two camps. Each side distrusted the other and struggled to increase its power and influence. This struggle rarely led to actual battle, or a hot war, so the conflict was generally known as the "Cold War."

One thing above all stopped the sides from fighting each other—the atomic bomb. In 1945, only the United States possessed a nuclear weapon, but by 1949 the Soviet Union had one as well. This was just the start of what became known as the "arms race." In 1952, the United States produced the hydrogen bomb, which produced a much more powerful explosion than the atomic bomb. Less than a year later, the

Soviet Union began making its own hydrogen bombs. By 1960, both sides were able to fire long-distance missiles armed with nuclear warheads.

In a panic, the Americans and Soviets built up huge stockpiles of these weapons and threatened that they were ready to use them if the other side fired first. Soon there were enough nuclear bombs to destroy Earth several times over. This horrifying situation was given a name—mutual assured destruction, or "MAD."

The horrible threat of nuclear war loomed over the world for 45 years after the end of World War II. The two sides had their fingers poised over the buttons that could send deadly missiles across the world. The slightest slip or moment of madness might have ended in the entire surface of Earth looking like Hiroshima and Nagasaki.

Soviet leader Nikita Khrushchev and U.S. President John F. Kennedy smiled for photographers as they arrived for a meeting on nuclear arms in Vienna, Austria, in 1961.

The Cold War ended in 1991 with the collapse of the Soviet Union, but the nuclear threat remained. Today, many countries all over the world had learned how to build their own atomic weapons. People also knew that terrorists could create small-scale bombs using the radioactive waste material from nuclear power plants.

Hiroshima and Nagasaki are still the only cities to have suffered the effects of nuclear warfare. Though they are now thriving cities (Hiroshima's population is more than 1 million and Nagasaki's is not far behind), they have never forgotten their special place in modern history. Today, both are centers for international peace campaigns, and people come from all over the world to visit their museums and monuments.

One of the most moving of all the memorials is the cenotaph in Hiroshima's Peace Park. On this monument are inscribed the names of those killed by the bomb. About 80,000 died on August 6, 1945, but the number of total deaths has never stopped rising since the bombing. The deadly curse of radiation continues to find victims. Today there are more than 180,000 names on the Hiroshima cenotaph.

WHO HAS NUCLEAR WEAPONS TODAY?	
Countries and Approxima Number of Weapons	
China	400
France	400
India	90
Israel	100
Pakistan	20
Russia	15,000
United Kingdom	200
United States (located in the U.S. and several countries in Europe)	12,000
TOTAL	30,000

Among them is the name of Sadako Sasaki. She was only 2 years old in 1945 and survived the blast. But later, as a schoolchild, Sadako fell ill with a blood cancer caused by the radiation. As she laid in a hospital, she decided to fold 1,000 paper cranes, which are a Japanese symbol of long life and good luck. Sadako finished her task, but she did not recover. She died in 1955, and a statue of her was erected in Hiroshima's Peace Park. Every day, visitors bring paper cranes to place next to the statue.

A Japanese woman marked the 55th anniversary of the Hiroshima bombing by launching paper lanterns on the Motoyasu River on August 6, 2000.

Every anniversary of the bombings of Hiroshima and Nagasaki reminds us of the fragility of the human race in a time in which the threat of nuclear war still exists. The remembrance of how hundreds of thousands of people lost their lives will continue to provide us with a solemn warning. ◢

85

Timeline

1758

Rudjer Boscovich of Croatia states that atoms are made up of smaller parts

1897

Joseph John Thomson of Great Britain discovers electrons

1905

Albert Einstein publishes his special theory of relativity

1911

Ernest Rutherford of New Zealand proposes that all atoms have a nucleus

1920

Rutherford proposes the existence of protons in atoms

1931

Japanese forces invade northern China

1932

James Chadwick discovers the neutron

1933

Adolf Hitler becomes leader of Germany; laws are passed persecuting Jews in Germany; Einstein and other scientists move to the West

1938

In Germany, Otto Hahn and Fritz Strassman create first example of nuclear fission

January 1939

Enrico Fermi moves from Italy to the United States; Lise Meitner and Otto Frisch confirm the splitting of atoms in the example of nuclear fission created by Hahn and Strassman

September 1939

World War II begins with German invasion of Poland

June 1940

Germans invade France

March 1941

New radioactive element plutonium discovered in the United States by Glenn Seaborg

April 1941

Japanese army approves research into atomic bomb

June 1941

Germans invade Soviet Union

December 1941

Japanese attack U.S. fleet in Pearl Harbor

March 1942

Japanese invade the Philippines, New Guinea, and Burma

June 1942

Japanese navy defeated by U.S. fleet at Midway

September 1942

The atomic bomb project is code-named the Manhattan Project

December 1942

Fermi masterminds construction of atomic pile at the University  of Chicago that creates the first sustainable chain reaction

March 1943

Robert Oppenheimer, the director of the U.S. atomic bomb project, arrives at the project's new headquarters in Los Alamos, New Mexico

Japanese navy gives up atomic bomb research

March 1944

U.S. troops regain Solomon Islands from the Japanese

June 1944

U.S. B-29s bomb Yawata in one of the first bombing raids on Japan itself

Allied forces invade northern France

Colonel Paul W. Tibbets given command of 509 Group on Tinian

March 10, 1945

U.S. B-29s make bombing raid on Tokyo, killing 100,000

April 12, 1945

 President Roosevelt dies; Harry S. Truman becomes president

May 7, 1945

Germany surrenders to Allied forces; end of war in Europe

May 25, 1945

Plan for Allied invasion of Japan drawn up

July 16, 1945

Trinity test explosion of nuclear device at Alamogordo, New Mexico

Little Boy bomb begins voyage by sea to Tinian

Timeline

July 26, 1945

Allies broadcast demand for Japanese surrender; Japanese reject it

July 31, 1945

Hiroshima chosen as the first target

August 6, 1945

 First atomic bomb dropped on Hiroshima from B-29 *Enola Gay*; about 80,000 are killed in the first few seconds

August 9, 1945

Second atomic bomb dropped on Nagasaki; about 45,000 killed or mortally injured immediately

August 15, 1945

Unconditional surrender of Japan; end of World War II

January 1946

Discussion group formed to tackle rebuilding of Hiroshima

August 1946

Quiet commemoration of first anniversary of the Hiroshima bombing

August 1947

Second anniversary celebrated with three-day Festival of Peace

May 1949

Japanese Parliament declares Hiroshima "City of Peace" and Nagasaki "City of International Culture"

October 1949

Soviet Union announces successful test of atomic bomb

June 1950

Korean War begins

August 1952

Memorial tower for victims of Hiroshima and Nagasaki unveiled

November 1952

U.S. researchers explode their first hydrogen bomb; the bomb is 700 times more powerful than Little Boy

July 1953

Korean War ends

1976

Japanese scientists begin thorough investigation of the damage caused by the bombing of Hiroshima and Nagasaki

ON THE WEB

For more information on *Hiroshima and Nagasaki*, use FactHound.

1 Go to *www.facthound.com*

2 Type in a search word related to this book or this book ID: 0756516218

3 Click on the *Fetch It* button. FactHound will find Web sites related to this book.

HISTORIC SITES

National Atomic Museum
1905 Mountain Road N.W.
Albuquerque, NM 87104
505/245-2137

The only museum of nuclear science and history in the United States to be chartered by Congress features exhibits and educational activities.

National Air and Space Museum
Steven F. Udvar-Hazy Center
14390 Air & Space Museum Parkway
Chantilly, VA 20151
202/633-1000

The museum houses thousands of space and aviation related artifacts. The B-29 *Enola Gay* went on display here in 2003.

LOOK FOR ALL THE BOOKS IN THIS SERIES

Glossary

bomb bay
the chamber in the belly of an aircraft where bombs are stored during flight; the bay has doors that open downward

bone marrow
the tissue at the center of our bones that helps form blood cells

capitalist
country or person practicing capitalism, an economic system in which goods and the ways of making them are owned by individuals or companies

carbon
an element that occurs in many forms, including in the air we breathe

cenotaph
a monument erected in honor of people who have died

chain reaction
a chemical reaction that sets off a series of similar changes; these continue until the material is used up

communist
a country or person practicing communism, a political system in which there is no private property and everything is owned and shared in common

dictator
a person who rules with complete authority, without political opposition or limits of power

electron
one of the tiny particles that move around the nucleus of an atom; electrons carry a negative electrical charge.

fission
the splitting of something into smaller parts

neutron
particle in the nucleus of an atom; neutrons contain no electrical charge.

nucleus
the central part of an atom, made up of neutrons and protons

particle
the basic unit that makes up an atom

physicist
a scientist who specializes in the study of matter and energy

plutonium
a silver radioactive element

proton
one of the particles in the nucleus of an atom; protons contain a positive electrical charge.

radiation
the waves or particles given off by radioactivity, which is the emission of particles from material that has unstable atomic nuclei or that is used in a nuclear reaction

uranium
a silvery-white element that is radioactive

Source Notes

Chapter 1

Page 10, line 12: Richard Rhodes. *The Making of the Atomic Bomb.* New York: Simon & Schuster, 1986, p. 709.

Page 10, line 26: Arata Osada, ed. *Children of the Atomic Bomb.* New York: HarperCollins, 1982, p. 305.

Page 10, line 28: Ibid., p. 307.

Page 12, line 2: Ibid., p. 306.

Page 12, sidebar: Adrian Weale. *Eyewitness Hiroshima.* London: Constable & Robinson, 1995, p. 215.

Page 13, line 11: *Children of the Atomic Bomb*, p. 305.

Chapter 2

Page 18, sidebar: *Eyewitness Hiroshima*, p. 232.

Chapter 3

Page 29, line 11: *The Making of the Atomic Bomb*, p. 316.

Page 31, sidebar: *Eyewitness Hiroshima*, p. 132.

Page 35, line 7: *The Making of the Atomic Bomb*, p. 713.

Chapter 4

Page 38, line 5: Ibid., p. 406.

Page 38, line 30: Ibid., p. 425.

Page 39, line 2: Ibid., p. 425.

Page 40, line 31: Ibid., p. 440.

Page 42, line 9: Leo Szilard. *Leo Szilard: His Version of the Facts.* Cambridge, Mass.: MIT Press, 1980, p. 146.

Page 42, line 24: *Eyewitness Hiroshima*, p. 159.

Page 46, sidebar: *The Making of the Atomic Bomb*, p. 520.

Page 48, line 18: Isidor Isaac Rabi. *Science: The Center of Culture.* New York: World Publishing Company, 1970, p. 138.

Page 48, line 24: Robert Jungk. *Brighter than a Thousand Suns.* New York: Harcourt Brace, 1958, p. 183.

Page 49, line 2: Leslie R. Groves. *Now It Can Be Told.* New York: Harper & Row, 1962, p. 298.

Page 49, line 3: *Eyewitness Hiroshima*, p. 166.

SOURCE NOTES

Chapter 5

Page 52, line 2: *The Making of the Atomic Bomb*, p. 696.

Page 54, line 22: *Eyewitness Hiroshima*, p. 233.

Page 57, lines 1–18: *Children of the Atomic Bomb*, p. 305.

Page 58, line 10: Michihiko Hachiya, M.D. *Hiroshima Diary: The Journal of a Japanese Physician, August 6–September 30, 1945: Fifty Years Later.* Chapel Hill: University of North Carolina Press, 1995, p. 18.

Chapter 6

Page 63, line 23: *Eyewitness Hiroshima*, p. 244.

Page 66, line 7: Ibid., p. 255.

Page 67, line 4: Ibid., p. 255.

Page 69, line 23: Ibid., p. 259.

Page 71, lines 13, 17: *Hiroshima Diary: The Journal of a Japanese Physician, August 6–September 30, 1945: Fifty Years Later*, p. 99.

Chapter 7

Page 75, line 27: *The Making of the Atomic Bomb*, p. 732.

Page 81, line 7: Official Homepage of Hiroshima Peace Memorial Museum. 22 Nov. 2005 <http://www.pcf.city.hiroshima.jp>

Select Bibliography

Groves, Leslie R. *Now It Can Be Told.* New York: Harper & Row, 1962.

Hachiya, Michihiko, M.D. *Hiroshima Diary: The Journal of a Japanese Physician, August 6–September 30, 1945: Fifty Years Later.* Chapel Hill: University of North Carolina Press, 1995.

Jungk, Robert. *Children of the Ashes: The Story of a Rebirth.* New York: Harcourt Brace, 1961.

Osada, Arata, ed. *Children of the Atomic Bomb.* New York: HarperCollins, 1982.

Rabi, Isidor Isaac. *Science: The Center of Culture.* New York: World Publishing Company, 1970.

Rhodes, Richard. *The Making of the Atomic Bomb.* New York: Simon & Schuster, 1986.

Szilard, Leo. *Leo Szilard: His Version of the Facts.* Cambridge, Mass.: MIT Press, 1980.

Thomas, Gordon, and Max Morgan Witts. *Ruin from the Air: The Atomic Mission to Hiroshima.* New York: HarperCollins, 1985.

Weale, Adrian. *Eyewitness Hiroshima.* London: Constable & Robinson, 1995.

Further Reading

Downing, David, and Nathaniel Harris. *Hiroshima: Witness to History.* Chicago: Heinemann Library, 2004.

Gonzales, Doreen. *The Manhattan Project and the Atomic Bomb in American History.* Berkeley Heights, N.J.: Enslow Publishers, 2002.

Malam, John. *The Bombing of Hiroshima: Date With History.* Mankato, Minn.: Smart Apple Media, 2002.

Mckain, Mark, ed. *Making and Using the Atomic Bomb.* San Diego: Greenhaven Press, 2002.

Index

ABOUT THE AUTHOR

Andrew Langley is the author of many history books for children. These include a biography of Mikhail Gorbachev, *The Roman News*, and *A Castle at War*, which was shortlisted for the Times Education Supplement Information Book Award. He lives in Wiltshire, England, with his family and two dogs.

IMAGE CREDITS

Corbis pp. **37**, **44** (Hulton-Deutsch) **62**, **65**, **70**, **74**, **76**, **78** (Bettmann), **81** (Michael S. Yamashita), **85** (Reuters), **30**, **43**, **68**; Getty 2005 p. **9**; Topfoto pp. **11**, **13**, **14-15** and **6** (PAL), **20** and **86** bottom right, **22**, **25** and **86** top right, **27**, **28** and **86** left, **41** and **87** left, **49**, **2** and **55** and **88**, **56**, **58-59**, **83**; United States National Archives and Records Administration pp. **50** (Harry S. Truman Library), **32-33** (NARA Pacific Region), **52** and **87** right, **61**, **66** and **cover**, **73**, **17**, **5** and **34**, **39**.